D1548708

FOR THE
FAITH

UNDERSTANDING AND PRACTICING THE FAITH
ONCE DELIVERED TO THE SAINTS

TIM CHRISTOSON

First published in 2007 by Striving Together Publications, a
ministry of Lancaster Baptist Church, Lancaster, CA 93535.
Striving Together Publications is committed to providing tried,
trusted, and proven books that will further equip local churches
to carry out the Great Commission. Your comments and
suggestions are valued.

Striving Together Publications
4020 E. Lancaster Blvd.
Lancaster, CA 93535
800.201.7748

Cover design by Jeremy Lofgren
Layout by Craig Parker
Edited by Maggie Ruhl
Special thanks to our proofreaders.

ISBN 978-1-59894-042-8

Printed in the United States of America

Table of Contents

The Significance of Our Faith

Key Verses

"Moreover, brethren, I declare unto you the gospel which I preached unto you, which also ye have received, and wherein ye stand; By which also ye are saved, if ye keep in memory what I preached unto you, unless ye have believed in vain. For I delivered unto you first of all that which I also received, how that Christ died for our sins according to the scriptures; And that he was buried, and that he rose again the third day according to the scriptures:"—1 CORINTHIANS 15:1–4

Lesson Overview

Sadly, many speakers and authors of twenty-first-century Christendom downplay the importance of Bible doctrine. Many Christians today attend church because of convenience or programs offered, rather than soundness of doctrine. In contrast, healthy Christians have always understood the importance of developing a working knowledge of the basic doctrines of the Christian faith.

Christians should appreciate the importance of maintaining doctrinal unity and purity as a local assembly. In this day of confusion, we have the opportunity to be shining lights of distinction and clarity.

Introduction

_____

_____

_____

I. The _____ of Our Faith

A. *Our faith has been preached* _____. *(v. 1)*
"*For the preaching of the cross is to them that perish foolishness; but unto us which are saved it is the power of God.*"—1 CORINTHIANS 1:18

_____

_____

B. *Our faith has been received* _____. *(v. 1)*
"*For unto us was the gospel preached, as well as unto them: but the word preached did not profit them, not being mixed with faith in them that heard it.*"
—HEBREWS 4:2

_____

_____

C. *Our faith has been verified* _____. *(v. 1)*
"*And what shall I more say? for the time would fail me to tell of Gedeon, and of Barak, and of Samson, and of Jephthae; of David also, and Samuel, and of the prophets: Who* **through faith** *subdued kingdoms, wrought righteousness, obtained promises, stopped the mouths of lions, Quenched the violence of fire, escaped the edge of the sword, out of weakness were made strong, waxed valiant in fight, turned to flight the armies of the*

aliens. And these all, having obtained a good report through faith..."—HEBREWS 11:32–34, 39

_____

_____

II. The _____ of Our Faith

"*For I delivered unto you first of all that which I also received, how that Christ died for our sins according to the scriptures; And that he was buried, and that he rose again the third day according to the scriptures: And that he was seen of Cephas, then of the twelve: After that, he was seen of above five hundred brethren at once; of whom the greater part remain unto this present, but some are fallen asleep. After that, he was seen of James; then of all the apostles. And last of all he was seen of me also, as of one born out of due time.*"—1 CORINTHIANS 15:3–8

A. Christ's _____ death (v. 3)

"*But God commendeth his love toward us, in that, while we were yet sinners, Christ died for us. Much more then, being now justified by his blood, we shall be saved from wrath through him. For if, when we were enemies, we were reconciled to God by the death of his Son, much more, being reconciled, we shall be saved by his life.*"
—ROMANS 5:8–10

_____

_____

B. Christ's _____ burial (v. 4)

"*Command therefore that the sepulchre be made sure until the third day, lest his disciples come by night, and steal him away, and say unto the people, He is risen from the dead: so the last error shall be worse than the first. Pilate said unto them, Ye have a watch: go your way, make it as sure as ye can. So they went, and made the sepulchre sure, sealing the stone, and setting a watch."*—MATTHEW 27:64–66

_____

_____

C. Christ's _____ resurrection (v. 4)

_____

_____

III. The _____ of Our Faith

A. Our _____ revolves around it.
"And if Christ be not risen, then is our preaching vain, and your faith is also vain. Yea, and we are found false witnesses of God; because we have testified of God that he raised up Christ: whom he raised not up, if so be that the dead rise not."—1 CORINTHIANS 15:14–15

_____

_____

B. Our _____ hinges on it.
"And if Christ be not raised, your faith is vain; ye are yet in your sins."—1 CORINTHIANS 15:17

_____

_____

C. Our _____ depends on it.
"Then they also which are fallen asleep in Christ are perished."—1 CORINTHIANS 15:18

"Behold, I shew you a mystery; We shall not all sleep, but we shall all be changed, In a moment, in the twinkling of an eye, at the last trump: for the trumpet shall sound, and the dead shall be raised incorruptible, and we shall be changed. For this corruptible must put on incorruption, and this mortal must put on immortality."—1 CORINTHIANS 15:51–53

_____

_____

D. Our _____ and _____ are found in it.

"If in this life only we have hope in Christ, we are of all men most miserable."—1 CORINTHIANS 15:19

"But thanks be to God, which giveth us the victory through our Lord Jesus Christ."—1 CORINTHIANS 15:57

_____

_____

IV. The _____ for Our Faith

"Therefore, my beloved brethren, be ye stedfast, unmoveable, always abounding in the work of the Lord, forasmuch as ye know that your labour is not in vain in the Lord."
—1 CORINTHIANS 15:58

A. Be _____.

_____

_____

B. Be _____.

_____

_____

C. *Always* _____ *in the work of the*
   Lord.

   _____

   _____

Conclusion

_____

_____

_____

Study Questions

1. According to 1 Peter 3:15, why is it important to know "*why* we believe what we believe"?

2. In Luke 11:32, how is the power of preaching shown?

3. Why was the preaching "not profitable" in Hebrews 4:2?

4. What are the three ingredients of our faith?

5. How does Christ's forgiveness hinge on our faith?

6. As Christians, we are to be steadfast in our faith— "settled in and firmly situated." Describe a Christian who has demonstrated steadfastness in his or her faith and describe qualities that make him or her that way.

    How can you learn from his or her example?

7. If you had to choose one personal weakness that the devil may use to tempt you to be "moveable" in your faith, what weakness would that be? (Ex: bitterness, money, pride, etc.)

    Whatever this weakness may be, ask the Lord to specifically give you grace and strength to keep you from the devil's temptations. (Memorize 1 Corinthians 10:13)

8. Paul challenged the Corinthian believers to err on the side of doing more for the cause of Christ instead of less. Take a moment to review your weekly schedule, and ask how you can do more for the work of the ministry.

    Name one ministry or area of service you can help with so that you may strive to be *always abounding in the work of the Lord.*

9. What does God promise in 1 Corinthians 15:58 if we remain steadfast, unmovable, and always abounding in the work of the Lord?

Memory Verses

"For I delivered unto you first of all that which I also received, how that Christ died for our sins according to the scriptures; And that he was buried, and that he rose again the third day according to the scriptures:"—1 CORINTHIANS 15:3–4

Our Faith in God's Word

Key Verses

"But continue thou in the things which thou hast learned and hast been assured of, knowing of whom thou hast learned them; And that from a child thou hast known the holy scriptures, which are able to make thee wise unto salvation through faith which is in Christ Jesus. All scripture is given by inspiration of God, and is profitable for doctrine, for reproof, for correction, for instruction in righteousness: That the man of God may be perfect, throughly furnished unto all good works."
—2 TIMOTHY 3:14–17

Lesson Overview

As Christians, we want to not only understand the process of receiving the Scriptures, but also strengthen our confidence in the Bible. If we truly understand the great lengths to which God went in order to communicate His Truth to mankind, we will respond by:

1. Giving His Word our *attention* through reading, memorizing, meditating, and placing a high priority on its teaching and preaching.
2. Giving His Word our *submission* through obedience and Scriptural living.

Introduction

_____

_____

_____

I. Our _____ of the Bible

A. The Bible began with a process called

_____.

"God, who at sundry times and in divers manners spake in time past unto the fathers by the prophets, Hath in these last days spoken unto us by his Son, whom he hath appointed heir of all things, by whom also he made the worlds;"—HEBREWS 1:1–2

"For this cause also thank we God without ceasing, because, when ye received the word of God which ye heard of us, ye received it not as the word of men, but as it is in truth, the word of God, which effectually worketh also in you that believe."—1 THESSALONIANS 2:13

_____

_____

B. The Bible was written down through a process called _____. (v. 16)

"Knowing this first, that no prophecy of the scripture is of any private interpretation. For the prophecy came not in old time by the will of man: but holy men of God spake as they were moved by the Holy Ghost."
—2 PETER 1:20–21

_____

_____

C. **The Bible has been delivered to us through a process called** _____.

"The words of the LORD are pure words: as silver tried in a furnace of earth, purified seven times. Thou shalt keep them, O LORD, thou shalt preserve them from this generation for ever."—PSALM 12:6–7

_____

_____

II. The _____ of the Bible

A. **The Bible's reliability is seen in its** _____.

"Every word of God is pure: he is a shield unto them that put their trust in him."—PROVERBS 30:5

_____

_____

B. **The Bible's reliability is seen in its**

_____.

"Thou shalt keep them, O Lord, thou shalt preserve them from this generation for ever."—PSALM 12:7

_____

_____

III. Our _____ to the Bible

A. **We should respond by _____ it.**

"Till I come, give attendance to reading, to exhortation, to doctrine."—1 TIMOTHY 4:13

"Cause me to hear thy lovingkindness in the morning; for in thee do I trust: cause me to know the way wherein I should walk; for I lift up my soul unto thee."—PSALM 143:8

B. We should respond by _____ on it.

"This book of the law shall not depart out of thy mouth; but thou shalt meditate therein day and night, that thou mayest observe to do according to all that is written therein: for then thou shalt make thy way prosperous, and then thou shalt have good success."
—JOSHUA 1:8

"Let the words of my mouth, and the meditation of my heart, be acceptable in thy sight, O Lord, my strength, and my redeemer."—PSALM 19:14

C. We should respond by _____ it.

"Thy word have I hid in mine heart, that I might not sin against thee."—PSALM 119:11

D. We should respond by _____ it preached and taught.

"But hath in due times manifested his word through preaching, which is committed unto me according to the commandment of God our Saviour;"—TITUS 1:3

"It seemed good unto us, being assembled with one accord, to send chosen men unto you with our beloved Barnabas and Paul,"—ACTS 15:25

———————————————————————————

———————————————————————————

E. We should respond by _____ it.
"But be ye doers of the word, and not hearers only, deceiving your own selves. For if any be a hearer of the word, and not a doer, he is like unto a man beholding his natural face in a glass: For he beholdeth himself, and goeth his way, and straightway forgetteth what manner of man he was. But whoso looketh into the perfect law of liberty, and continueth therein, he being not a forgetful hearer, but a doer of the work, this man shall be blessed in his deed."—JAMES 1:22–25

———————————————————————————

———————————————————————————

Conclusion

———————————————————————————

———————————————————————————

———————————————————————————

Study Questions

1. Define the term *revelation.*

2. Explain the process of inspiration.

3. List two verses in the Bible where God promises to preserve His Word.

4. How can we meditate upon God's Word?

5. What are some practical ways to make meditating upon God's Word (Psalm 119:97) a reality in your life?

6. List three methods that will help you memorize Scripture on a daily basis.

7. Begin memorizing Scriptures by topic. The following three verses are on the topic of grace. Work to have these memorized by the next lesson: James 4:6, Ephesians 2:8, and Hebrews 4:16.

8. List three things to which God likens His Word.

9. If you do not already have a systematic way of reading your Bible, begin to make a schedule for your daily Bible reading. Your schedule may consist of reading a Proverb a day, or it may consist of reading 3–4 chapters a day in order to finish reading the Bible in a year.

Memory Verse

"All scripture is given by inspiration of God, and is profitable for doctrine, for reproof, for correction, for instruction in righteousness:"—2 TIMOTHY 3:16

Our Faith in God

Key Verses

"*Praise ye the* LORD. *Praise, O ye servants of the* LORD, *praise the name of the* LORD. *Blessed be the name of the* LORD *from this time forth and for evermore. From the rising of the sun unto the going down of the same the* LORD's *name is to be praised. The* LORD *is high above all nations, and his glory above the heavens. Who is like unto the* LORD *our God, who dwelleth on high, Who humbleth himself to behold the things that are in heaven, and in the earth! He raiseth up the poor out of the dust, and lifteth the needy out of the dunghill; That he may set him with princes, even with the princes of his people. He maketh the barren woman to keep house, and to be a joyful mother of children. Praise ye the* LORD."—PSALM 113

Lesson Overview

Having an understanding of the character and personality of the God of the Bible is vitally important to being grounded in the faith. It is not uncommon to hear something like, "All religions worship the same God—they just call Him by different names." While this statement may be uttered by sincere lips, it is absolutely incorrect.

God's people should strive to understand that the God we worship as Bible-believing Christians has revealed Himself in His Word and will not allow Himself to be confused with false gods.

Introduction

_____

_____

_____

I. We Worship a _____ God

"God hath spoken once; twice have I heard this; that power belongeth unto God."—PSALM 62:11

A. His power is seen in His _____ creation.

"The heavens declare the glory of God; and the firmament sheweth his handywork."—PSALM 19:1

"By the word of the LORD were the heavens made; and all the host of them by the breath of his mouth." —PSALM 33:6

_____

_____

B. His power is seen in His _____.

"Both riches and honour come of thee, and thou reignest over all; and in thine hand is power and might; and in thine hand it is to make great, and to give strength unto all."—1 CHRONICLES 29:12

_____

_____

C. His power is seen in His _____.

1. He is able to do anything—_____.

"I know that thou canst do every thing, and that no thought can be withholden from thee."—JOB 42:2

"But Jesus beheld them, and said unto them, With men this is impossible; but with God all things are possible."—MATTHEW 19:26

2. **He knows everything—**_____.

"For if our heart condemn us, God is greater than our heart, and knoweth all things."—1 JOHN 3:20

3. **He is everywhere—**_____.

"The eyes of the LORD are in every place, beholding the evil and the good."—PROVERBS 15:3

"Can any hide himself in secret places that I shall not see him? saith the LORD. Do not I fill heaven and earth? saith the LORD."—JEREMIAH 23:24

_____

_____

II. We Worship a _____ God

"As for God, his way is perfect: the word of the LORD is tried: he is a buckler to all those that trust in him."
—PSALM 18:30

A. *He is perfect in His* _____.

"For though there be that are called gods, whether in heaven or in earth, (as there be gods many, and lords many,) But to us there is but one God, the Father, of whom are all things, and we in him; and one Lord Jesus Christ, by whom are all things, and we by him."
—1 CORINTHIANS 8:5–6

_____

_____

B. He is perfect in His _____.
"Exalt the LORD *our God, and worship at his holy hill; for the* LORD *our God is holy."*—PSALM 99:9

"Because it is written, Be ye holy; for I am holy."
—1 PETER 1:16

_____

_____

C. He is perfect in His _____
and justice.
"...Shall not the Judge of all the earth do right?"
—GENESIS 18:25

"He is the Rock, his work is perfect: for all his ways are judgment: a God of truth and without iniquity, just and right is he."—DEUTERONOMY 32:4

_____

_____

D. He is perfect in His _____.
"For I am the LORD, *I change not..."*—MALACHI 3:6

"Jesus Christ the same yesterday, and to day, and for ever."—HEBREWS 13:8

_____ .

_____

III. We Worship a _____ God

"For I know the thoughts that I think toward you, saith the LORD, *thoughts of peace, and not of evil, to give you an expected end."*—JEREMIAH 29:11

A. *His personality is seen in His* _____.

1. God

"In the beginning God created the heaven and the earth."—GENESIS 1:1

2. I Am

"And God said unto Moses, I AM THAT I AM: and he said, Thus shalt thou say unto the children of Israel, I AM hath sent me unto you."—EXODUS 3:14

3. Jehovah

"And I appeared unto Abraham, unto Isaac, and unto Jacob, by the name of God Almighty, but by my name JEHOVAH was I not known to them."—EXODUS 6:3

4. The God of gods and Lord of lords

"For the LORD your God is God of gods, and Lord of lords, a great God, a mighty, and a terrible, which regardeth not persons, nor taketh reward:"—DEUTERONOMY 10:17

5. Heavenly Father

"Behold the fowls of the air: for they sow not, neither do they reap, nor gather into barns; yet your heavenly Father feedeth them. Are ye not much better than they?"—MATTHEW 6:26

_____

_____

B. His personality is seen in His _____.

"For there are three that bear record in heaven, the Father, the Word, and the Holy Ghost: and these three are one."—1 JOHN 5:7

_____

_____

C. His personality is seen in His _____ care.

"But God, who is rich in mercy, for his great love wherewith he loved us, That in the ages to come he might shew the exceeding riches of his grace in his kindness toward us through Christ Jesus."—EPHESIANS 2:4, 7

"Casting all your care upon him; for he careth for you."—1 PETER 5:7

_____

_____

Conclusion

_____

_____

_____

Study Questions

1. Describe two ways we should respond to our relationship with God.

2. Describe how God's power is shown through creation.

3. What term is sometimes used to describe God's authority?

4. According to the Scriptures, define the following three terms that describe God: omnipotence, omniscience, and omnipresence.

5. What should God's holiness create in the life of every believer?

6. How does the one, true God contrast with false gods?

7. List three of God's titles given in the Bible.

8. Knowing that the great God in Heaven cares for you personally, according to 1 Peter 5:7, how are you supposed to respond to His care?

9. You may know all about God, but what steps have you taken in the past week to better know God personally? What steps can you take this upcoming week to better know God and build your relationship with Him?

Memory Verse

"Thou art worthy, O Lord, to receive glory and honour and power: for thou hast created all things, and for thy pleasure they are and were created."—REVELATION 4:11

Our Faith in God's Son

Key Verses

"When Jesus came into the coasts of Caesarea Philippi, he asked his disciples, saying, Whom do men say that I the Son of man am? And they said, Some say that thou art John the Baptist: some, Elias; and others, Jeremias, or one of the prophets. He saith unto them, But whom say ye that I am? And Simon Peter answered and said, Thou art the Christ, the Son of the living God. And Jesus answered and said unto him, Blessed art thou, Simon Barjona: for flesh and blood hath not revealed it unto thee, but my Father which is in heaven."
—MATTHEW 16:13–17

Lesson Overview

Liberal denominations have compromised their position on the uniqueness of God's Son. In addition, Jesus Himself warned that false teachers would come into the world proclaiming that they are Christ, and many have done so. Further, cults teach a variety of heretical teachings under the guise of belief in the Christ of the Bible.

These are days for Christ's followers to know what they believe about Him, to know why they believe it, and to grow increasingly deeper in their relationship with Him.

Introduction

_____

_____

_____

I. The _____ of Jesus Christ

A. *He is _____ with God the Father.*
"*Who, being in the form of God, thought it not robbery to be equal with God:*"—PHILIPPIANS 2:6

"*Therefore the Jews sought the more to kill him, because he not only had broken the sabbath, but said also that God was his Father, making himself equal with God.*"—JOHN 5:18

_____

_____

B. *He is the _____ image of God.*
"*Who is the image of the invisible God, the firstborn of every creature: For by him were all things created, that are in heaven, and that are in earth, visible and invisible, whether they be thrones, or dominions, or principalities, or powers: all things were created by him, and for him:*"—COLOSSIANS 1:15–16

_____

_____

C. *He is eternally _____.*
"*And he is before all things, and by him all things consist.*"—COLOSSIANS 1:17

"In the beginning was the Word, and the Word was with God, and the Word was God. The same was in the beginning with God."—JOHN 1:1–2

_____

_____

II. The _____ of Jesus Christ

"And Thomas answered and said unto him, My Lord and my God."—JOHN 20:28

"But unto the Son he saith, Thy throne, O God, is for ever and ever: a sceptre of righteousness is the sceptre of thy kingdom."—HEBREWS 1:8

A. The _____ of Jesus express His deity.

"I and my Father are one. Then the Jews took up stones again to stone him. Jesus answered them, Many good works have I shewed you from my Father; for which of those works do ye stone me? The Jews answered him, saying, For a good work we stone thee not; but for blasphemy; and because that thou, being a man, makest thyself God."—JOHN 10:30–33

_____

_____

B. The _____ of Jesus exhibit His deity.

1. Jesus created the world.

"All things were made by him; and without him was not any thing made that was made."—JOHN 1:3

"For by him were all things created, that are in heaven, and that are in earth, visible and invisible,

whether they be thrones, or dominions, or principalities, or powers: all things were created by him, and for him:"—COLOSSIANS 1:16

2. Jesus exercised authority over nature.

"And he arose, and rebuked the wind, and said unto the sea, Peace, be still. And the wind ceased, and there was a great calm. And he said unto them, Why are ye so fearful? how is it that ye have no faith? And they feared exceedingly, and said one to another, What manner of man is this, that even the wind and the sea obey him?"
—MARK 4:39–41

3. Jesus exercised power over human disease.

"And a woman having an issue of blood twelve years, which had spent all her living upon physicians, neither could be healed of any, Came behind him, and touched the border of his garment: and immediately her issue of blood stanched. And he said unto her, Daughter, be of good comfort: thy faith hath made thee whole; go in peace."
—LUKE 8:43–44, 48

4. Jesus granted the forgiveness of sins.

"When Jesus saw their faith, he said unto the sick of the palsy, Son, thy sins be forgiven thee. But there were certain of the scribes sitting there, and reasoning in their hearts, Why doth this man thus speak blasphemies? who can forgive sins but God only?"—MARK 2:5–7

5. Jesus conquered death and the grave!

"Knowing that Christ being raised from the dead dieth no more; death hath no more dominion over him."—ROMANS 6:9

_____

_____

C. The _____ of the Scriptures _____ His deity.

"In the beginning was the Word, and the Word was with God, and the Word was God. And the Word was made flesh, and dwelt among us, (and we beheld his glory, the glory as of the only begotten of the Father,) full of grace and truth."—JOHN 1:1, 14

_____

_____

III. The _____ of Jesus Christ

A. The _____

"Grace be to you, and peace, from God our Father, and from the Lord Jesus Christ."—EPHESIANS 1:2

_____

_____

B. The _____

"And we know that the Son of God is come, and hath given us an understanding, that we may know him that is true, and we are in him that is true, even in his Son Jesus Christ. This is the true God, and eternal life."—1 JOHN 5:20

"But grow in grace, and in the knowledge of our Lord and Saviour Jesus Christ. To him be glory both now and for ever. Amen."—2 PETER 3:18

_____

_____

C. **The _____ of God**

"The next day John seeth Jesus coming unto him, and saith, Behold the Lamb of God, which taketh away the sin of the world."—JOHN 1:29

_____

_____

D. **The _____ of God**

"The beginning of the gospel of Jesus Christ, the Son of God;"—MARK 1:1

_____

_____

E. **The First and the Last, the _____ and**

_____

"I am Alpha and Omega, the beginning and the end, the first and the last."—REVELATION 22:13

_____

_____

F. **The _____ Shepherd, the _____ Shepherd**

"I am the good shepherd: the good shepherd giveth his life for the sheep."—JOHN 10:11

"And when the chief Shepherd shall appear, ye shall receive a crown of glory that fadeth not away."—1 PETER 5:4

_____

_____

IV. The _____ of Jesus Christ

A. He desires _____—He wants all people to be saved.

"For the Son of man is come to seek and to save that which was lost."—LUKE 19:10

"For this is good and acceptable in the sight of God our Saviour; Who will have all men to be saved, and to come unto the knowledge of the truth." —1 TIMOTHY 2:3–4

_____

_____

B. He desires _____—He wants us to spend time with Him.

"Abide in me, and I in you. As the branch cannot bear fruit of itself, except it abide in the vine; no more can ye, except ye abide in me. As the Father hath loved me, so have I loved you: continue ye in my love." —JOHN 15:4, 9

_____

_____

C. He desires _____—He wants to bless and use each of our lives.

"The thief cometh not, but for to steal, and to kill, and to destroy: I am come that they might have life, and that they might have it more abundantly." —JOHN 10:10

"I am the vine, ye are the branches: He that abideth in me, and I in him, the same bringeth forth much fruit: for without me ye can do nothing. Herein is my Father *glorified, that ye bear much fruit; so shall ye be my disciples."*—John 15:5, 8

"Now unto him that is able to do exceeding abundantly above all that we ask or think, according to the power that worketh in us,"—Ephesians 3:20

_____

_____

Conclusion

_____

_____

_____

Study Questions

1. In John 5:18, Jesus Christ usurped authority over the Jews. How did they respond to His proclaiming equality with God?

2. What was the significance of Jesus' receiving the worship of Thomas?

3. Read John 1:1 and 14. In your own words explain how these verses support Christ's deity.

4. In John 10, Jesus was threatened with being stoned for claiming to be one with God. Describe a time when you felt threatened to speak of your relationship with God.

5. In Luke 19:10, how does Jesus demonstrate His desire to see *all* come to repentance?

6. Why do we need to have a relationship with Christ according to John 15:4 and 9?

7. In John 15:8, describe how the Father is glorified in our lives.

8. Take a moment and describe your testimony—the time you accepted Jesus Christ as your Saviour.

9. Have you developed an unwavering commitment to the Person of Jesus Christ? List three ways that your commitment to Christ is seen in your life.

Memory Verse

"Jesus Christ the same yesterday, and to day, and for ever."
—HEBREWS 13:8

Our Faith in the Holy Spirit

Key Verses

"Nevertheless I tell you the truth; It is expedient for you that I go away: for if I go not away, the Comforter will not come unto you; but if I depart, I will send him unto you. And when he is come, he will reprove the world of sin, and of righteousness, and of judgment: Of sin, because they believe not on me; Of righteousness, because I go to my Father, and ye see me no more; Of judgment, because the prince of this world is judged. I have yet many things to say unto you, but ye cannot bear them now. Howbeit when he, the Spirit of truth, is come, he will guide you into all truth: for he shall not speak of himself; but whatsoever he shall hear, that shall he speak: and he will shew you things to come. He shall glorify me: for he shall receive of mine, and shall shew it unto you."—JOHN 16:7–14

Lesson Overview

Appreciating the importance of the Holy Spirit and responding to His conviction is an essential component in this lesson. Our constant prayer should be for the Holy Spirit to give us victory over the flesh, to grant us power to witness, and to enable us to reach our full potential in Christ.

The ministry and presence of the Holy Spirit must become a daily reality in our lives!

Introduction

_____

_____

_____

I. The _____ of the Holy Spirit

A. He was sent by Jesus Christ upon His _____.

"Nevertheless I tell you the truth; It is expedient for you that I go away: for if I go not away, the Comforter will not come unto you; but if I depart, I will send him unto you."—JOHN 16:7

_____

_____

B. He was sent to _____ to and through Christ's followers.

1. To _____ them

2. To _____ them

   "But the Comforter, which is the Holy Ghost, whom the Father will send in my name, he shall teach you all things, and bring all things to your remembrance, whatsoever I have said unto you."—JOHN 14:26

3. To _____ Jesus

   "He shall glorify me: for he shall receive of mine, and shall shew it unto you."—JOHN 16:14

II. The _____ of the Holy Spirit

A. *His attributes express _____.*

1. He is eternally _____.

   *"How much more shall the blood of Christ, who through the **eternal Spirit** offered himself without spot to God, purge your conscience from dead works to serve the living God?"*—HEBREWS 9:14

2. He is _____—everywhere at once.

   *"Whither shall I go from **thy spirit**? or whither shall I flee from thy presence? If I ascend up into heaven, thou art there: if I make my bed in hell, behold, thou art there. If I take the wings of the morning, and dwell in the uttermost parts of the sea; Even there shall thy hand lead me, and thy right hand shall hold me."*—PSALM 139:7–10

3. He is _____—all powerful.

   *"And the angel answered and said unto her, **The Holy Ghost** shall come upon thee, and **the power of the Highest** shall overshadow thee..."*—LUKE 1:35

4. He is _____—all knowing.

   "But God hath revealed them unto us by his Spirit: for the Spirit searcheth all things, yea, the deep things of God. For what man knoweth the things of a man, save the spirit of man which is in him? even so the things of God knoweth no man, but the Spirit of God."—1 CORINTHIANS 2:10–11

5. He imparts _____.

*"But if **the Spirit of him that raised up Jesus from the dead** dwell in you, he that raised up Christ from the dead shall also quicken your mortal bodies by his Spirit that dwelleth in you."*—ROMANS 8:11

6. He _____ the Scriptures.

"For the prophecy came not in old time by the will of man: but holy men of God spake as they were moved by the Holy Ghost."—2 PETER 1:21

B. *His attributes exhibit _____.*

1. He _____ the characteristics of a person.

2. He _____ the actions of a person.

3. He _____ the treatment of a person.

III. The _____ of the Holy Spirit

A. *The Holy Spirit is at work in the _____ at large.*

1. He _____ with mankind, restraining sin.

2. He _____ mankind.

3. He _____ to mankind.

"And we are his witnesses of these things; and so is also the Holy Ghost, whom God hath given to them that obey him."—ACTS 5:32

B. *The Holy Spirit is at work when someone* _____ .

1. The Holy Spirit _____ our spirit.

"Not by works of righteousness which we have done, but according to his mercy he saved us, by the washing of regeneration, and renewing of the Holy Ghost;"—TITUS 3:5

"Verily, verily, I say unto you, He that heareth my word, and believeth on him that sent me, hath everlasting life, and shall not come into condemnation; but is passed from death unto life."—JOHN 5:24

2. The Holy Spirit _____ us into the body of Christ.

"For by one Spirit are we all baptized into one body, whether we be Jews or Gentiles, whether we be bond or free; and have been all made to drink into one Spirit."—1 CORINTHIANS 12:13

"At that day ye shall know that I am in my Father, and ye in me, and I in you."—JOHN 14:20

"There is therefore now no condemnation to them which are in Christ Jesus, who walk not after the flesh, but after the Spirit."—ROMANS 8:1

3. **The Holy Spirit _____ us.**

   "In whom ye also trusted, after that ye heard the word of truth, the gospel of your salvation: in whom also after that ye believed, ye were sealed with that holy Spirit of promise, Which is the earnest of our inheritance until the redemption of the purchased possession, unto the praise of his glory."—EPHESIANS 1:13–14

4. **The Holy Spirit _____ us.**

   "But ye are not in the flesh, but in the Spirit, if so be that the Spirit of God dwell in you. Now if any man have not the Spirit of Christ, he is none of his."—ROMANS 8:9

   "Know ye not that ye are the temple of God, and that the Spirit of God dwelleth in you?"—1 CORINTHIANS 3:16

5. **The Holy Spirit _____ us.**

C. *The Holy Spirit is at work in the _____ of Christians.*

1. **He will _____ us, if we yield to Him.**

   "This I say then, Walk in the Spirit, and ye shall not fulfil the lust of the flesh. For the flesh lusteth against the Spirit, and the Spirit against the flesh: and these are contrary the one to the other: so that ye cannot do the things that ye would. But if ye be led of the Spirit, ye are not under the law."—GALATIANS 5:16–18

2. He will _____ us, if we hear Him.

    "But the anointing which ye have received of him abideth in you, and ye need not that any man teach you: but as the same anointing teacheth you of all things, and is truth, and is no lie, and even as it hath taught you, ye shall abide in him." —1 JOHN 2:27

3. He will _____ us, if we submit to Him.

    "That he would grant you, according to the riches of his glory, to be strengthened with might by his Spirit in the inner man;" —EPHESIANS 3:16

4. He will _____ us, if we will follow Him.

    "For as many as are led by the Spirit of God, they are the sons of God." —ROMANS 8:14

5. He will _____ us, if we ask Him.

    "But ye shall receive power, after that the Holy Ghost is come upon you…" —ACTS 1:8

6. He will _____ through us, if we allow Him.

    "And hope maketh not ashamed; because the love of God is shed abroad in our hearts by the Holy Ghost which is given unto us." —ROMANS 5:5

7. He will _____ us, if we are sensitive to Him.

    "And he that keepeth his commandments dwelleth in him, and he in him. And hereby we know that

he abideth in us, by the Spirit which he hath given us."—1 JOHN 3:24

8. **He will _____ us, if we avail ourselves of Him.**

   "And be not drunk with wine, wherein is excess; but be filled with the Spirit;"—EPHESIANS 5:18

Conclusion

_____

_____

_____

Study Questions

1. Picture yourself as one of Jesus' disciples. How would you have felt and responded to the news that He was going away, and He was leaving you with His Spirit?

2. In John 16:7, why was it expedient for Jesus to go away?

3. What did Jesus refer to the Holy Spirit as four times in John 14–16, and what does this word mean?

   Read John 14–16, and point out the times Jesus Christ refers to the Holy Spirit.

4. List and describe the three attributes of the Holy Spirit.

5. In John 16:8, the Bible speaks of the Holy Spirit reproving the world for sin. Describe the last time you felt conviction from the Holy Spirit. How did you respond to this conviction?

6.   Acts 5:32 explains how the Holy Ghost witnesses to mankind. How can His witnessing help your soulwinning efforts?

7.   What are the five actions that occur every time someone receives Christ?

8.   What is the difference between being indwelled with the Holy Spirit and having the filling of the Holy Spirit?

9.   In what ways can you quench the Holy Spirit in your life? How can you resist the quenching of the Holy Spirit's working through you?

Memory Verse

"And be not drunk with wine, wherein is excess; but be filled with the Spirit;"—EPHESIANS 5:18

LESSON SIX

The Faith That Saves Us

Key Verse

"Therefore we ought to give the more earnest heed to the things which we have heard, lest at any time we should let them slip. For if the word spoken by angels was stedfast, and every transgression and disobedience received a just recompence of reward; How shall we escape, if we neglect so great salvation; which at the first began to be spoken by the Lord, and was confirmed unto us by them that heard him;"—HEBREWS 2:1–3

Lesson Overview

In this day of confusion, Christians must understand the truth of God's Word regarding the doctrine of salvation. It is vitally important to equip every saint with scriptural truths, which can be used in witnessing to coworkers, friends, and relatives. Through study, Christians can prepare to answer people's questions about God's saving grace, using the authority of the Bible.

Salvation points to the core of God's love—the gift of His Son on the Cross. The truths in this lesson enable Christians to make a difference with their lives each day.

Introduction

_____

_____

_____

I. The _____ That _____ Our Salvation

A. All mankind is _____ and in need of salvation.

"Wherefore, as by one man sin entered into the world, and death by sin; and so death passed upon all men, for that all have sinned:"—ROMANS 5:12

_____

_____

B. Jesus provides the _____ way of salvation.

"Neither is there salvation in any other: for there is none other name under heaven given among men, whereby we must be saved."—ACTS 4:12

_____

_____

C. Salvation is received by _____, through _____, without _____.

"And if by grace, then is it no more of works: otherwise grace is no more grace. But if it be of works, then is it no more grace: otherwise work is no more work."
—ROMANS 11:6

_____

_____

D. Once received, our salvation is _____ and secure.

"My sheep hear my voice, and I know them, and they follow me: And I give unto them eternal life; and they shall never perish, neither shall any man pluck them out of my hand. My Father, which gave them me, is greater than all; and no man is able to pluck them out of my Father's hand."—JOHN 10:27–29

_____

_____

II. The _____ That _____ Our Salvation

A. _____

"For Christ also hath once suffered for sins, the just for the unjust, that he might bring us to God, being put to death in the flesh, but quickened by the Spirit:"—1 PETER 3:18

_____

_____

B. _____

"And all things are of God, who hath reconciled us to himself by Jesus Christ, and hath given to us the ministry of reconciliation; To wit, that God was in Christ, reconciling the world unto himself, not imputing their trespasses unto them; and hath committed unto us the word of reconciliation."—2 CORINTHIANS 5:18–19

_____

_____

C. _____

"And he is the propitiation for our sins: and not for ours only, but also for the sins of the whole world." —1 JOHN 2:2

_____

_____

D. _____

"For this is my blood of the new testament, which is shed for many for the remission of sins."—MATTHEW 26:28

_____

_____

E. _____

"Not by works of righteousness which we have done, but according to his mercy he saved us, by the washing of regeneration, and renewing of the Holy Ghost;" —TITUS 3:5

_____

_____

F. _____

"Christ hath redeemed us from the curse of the law, being made a curse for us: for it is written, Cursed is every one that hangeth on a tree:"—GALATIANS 3:13

_____

_____

G. _____

"Even as David also describeth the blessedness of the man, unto whom God imputeth righteousness without works, Saying, Blessed are they whose iniquities are forgiven, and whose sins are covered. Blessed is

the man to whom the Lord will not impute sin."
—ROMANS 4:6–8

_____

_____

H. _____

"For ye have not received the spirit of bondage again to fear; but ye have received the Spirit of adoption, whereby we cry, Abba, Father. The Spirit itself beareth witness with our spirit, that we are the children of God: And if children, then heirs; heirs of God, and joint-heirs with Christ; if so be that we suffer with him, that we may be also glorified together."—ROMANS 8:15–17

_____

_____

I. _____

"Therefore being justified by faith, we have peace with God through our Lord Jesus Christ:"—ROMANS 5:1

_____

_____

III. The _____ That _____ Our Salvation

A. The _____ tense of salvation

"For then must he often have suffered since the foundation of the world: but now once in the end of the world hath he appeared to put away sin by the sacrifice of himself."—HEBREWS 9:26

_____

_____

B. The _____ tense of salvation

"God forbid. How shall we, that are dead to sin, live any longer therein? Let not sin therefore reign in your mortal body, that ye should obey it in the lusts thereof. For sin shall not have dominion over you: for ye are not under the law, but under grace."—ROMANS 6:2, 12, 14

_____

_____

C. The _____ tense of salvation

"Who shall change our vile body, that it may be fashioned like unto his glorious body, according to the working whereby he is able even to subdue all things unto himself."—PHILIPPIANS 3:21

_____

_____

Consider the following diagram:

So Great Salvation • Hebrews 2:3		
Past	*Present*	*Future*
I have been saved from the **penalty** of sin. Romans 5:21	**I am being** saved from the **power** of sin. Romans 6:14	**I will be** saved from the **presence** of sin. 1 John 3:2
Justification Romans 5:1	**Sanctification** 1 Thessalonians 4:3	**Glorification** Philippians 3:21
Jesus appeared on **Calvary** for me. Hebrews 9:26	Jesus appears in **Heaven** for me. Hebrews 4:14–16	Jesus will appear in the **clouds** for me. Hebrews 9:28

Conclusion

Study Questions

1. Why is mankind in need of salvation?

2. Some sincere people would say that it does not really matter who or what you believe in, as long as you believe in someone or something. According to the Scriptures, how is this thinking wrong?

3. Why can't "being a good person" get you into Heaven?

4. Once saved, can you ever lose your salvation? Support your answer with a verse.

5. When you doubt your salvation, what should you do?

6. Define the word *substitution* according to this lesson.

7. What does Matthew 26:28 mean when referring to the "remission of sins"?

8. God's intent is that your salvation would play a meaningful role in your everyday life! Describe how you can conform to Christ's image every day—and thus make salvation a continual reality.

9. Take a quiet moment, and write a prayer of gratitude to the Lord for His gift of "so great salvation." Ask for His strength as you include names of people with whom you can share His gift.

Memory Verse

"Jesus saith unto him, I am the way, the truth, and the life: no man cometh unto the Father, but by me."—JOHN 14:6

When Our Faith Becomes Sight

Key Verses

"Let not your heart be troubled: ye believe in God, believe also in me. In my Father's house are many mansions: if it were not so, I would have told you. I go to prepare a place for you. And if I go and prepare a place for you, I will come again, and receive you unto myself; that where I am, there ye may be also."—JOHN 14:1–3

Lesson Overview

It is important for Christians to have an understanding of future events as they are described in God's Word. Having this understanding will inspire confidence in believers' hearts—motivating them to witness to those around them and encouraging them toward faithful Christian living.

Most twenty-first century Christians are either disinterested in prophecy or too intimidated by the topic to attempt to learn it. However, a simple study of future events should inspire and challenge each of us to be who God wants us to be in light of His grand plan.

Introduction

_____

_____

_____

I. The _____ of God's _____

A. The _____ on prophecy in God's Word

"Remember the former things of old: for I am God, and
there is none else; I am God, and there is none like
me, Declaring the end from the beginning, and from
ancient times the things that are not yet done, saying,
My counsel shall stand, and I will do all my pleasure:
Calling a ravenous bird from the east, the man that
executeth my counsel from a far country: yea, I have
spoken it, I will also bring it to pass; I have purposed it,
I will also do it."—ISAIAH 46:9–11

_____

_____

B. The _____ of prophecy in God's Word

"But the prophet, which shall presume to speak a word
in my name, which I have not commanded him to
speak, or that shall speak in the name of other gods,
even that prophet shall die. And if thou say in thine
heart, How shall we know the word which the Lord
hath not spoken? When a prophet speaketh in the name
of the LORD, if the thing follow not, nor come to pass,
that is the thing which the LORD hath not spoken, but
the prophet hath spoken it presumptuously: thou shalt
not be afraid of him."—DEUTERONOMY 18:20–22

_____

_____

II. The _____ of God's _____

A. The _____ of believers

"For this we say unto you by the word of the Lord, that we which are alive and remain unto the coming of the Lord shall not prevent them which are asleep. For the Lord himself shall descend from heaven with a shout, with the voice of the archangel, and with the trump of God: and the dead in Christ shall rise first: Then we which are alive and remain shall be caught up together with them in the clouds, to meet the Lord in the air: and so shall we ever be with the Lord."
—1 THESSALONIANS 4:15–17

_____

_____

B. The _____ of Christ for believers

"We are confident, I say, and willing rather to be absent from the body, and to be present with the Lord. Wherefore we labour, that, whether present or absent, we may be accepted of him. For we must all appear before the judgment seat of Christ; that every one may receive the things done in his body, according to that he hath done, whether it be good or bad."
—2 CORINTHIANS 5:8–10

_____

_____

C. The seven years of _____ on Earth

"For then shall be great tribulation, such as was not since the beginning of the world to this time, no, nor ever shall be."—MATTHEW 24:21

_____

_____

D. The _____ of Jesus Christ with His people

"Immediately after the tribulation of those days shall the sun be darkened, and the moon shall not give her light, and the stars shall fall from heaven, and the powers of the heavens shall be shaken: And then shall appear the sign of the Son of man in heaven: and then shall all the tribes of the earth mourn, and they shall see the Son of man coming in the clouds of heaven with power and great glory."—MATTHEW 24:29–30

_____

_____

E. The millennial _____ on Earth

"And I saw thrones, and they sat upon them, and judgment was given unto them: and I saw the souls of them that were beheaded for the witness of Jesus, and for the word of God, and which had not worshipped the beast, neither his image, neither had received his mark upon their foreheads, or in their hands; and they lived and reigned with Christ a thousand years."
—REVELATION 20:4

_____

_____

F. The final judgment of _____

"And when the thousand years are expired, Satan shall be loosed out of his prison, And shall go out to deceive the nations which are in the four quarters of the earth, Gog and Magog, to gather them together to battle: the number of whom is as the sand of the sea. And they went up on the breadth of the earth, and compassed the camp of the saints about, and the beloved city: and fire came down from God out of heaven, and devoured

them. And the devil that deceived them was cast into the lake of fire and brimstone, where the beast and the false prophet are, and shall be tormented day and night for ever and ever."—REVELATION 20:7–10

G. The _____ Throne Judgment

"And I saw a great white throne, and him that sat on it, from whose face the earth and the heaven fled away; and there was found no place for them. And I saw the dead, small and great, stand before God; and the books were opened: and another book was opened, which is the book of life: and the dead were judged out of those things which were written in the books, according to their works. And the sea gave up the dead which were in it; and death and hell delivered up the dead which were in them: and they were judged every man according to their works. And death and hell were cast into the lake of fire. This is the second death. And whosoever was not found written in the book of life was cast into the lake of fire."—REVELATION 20:11–15

H. Beginning of _____ and the new Heaven and Earth

"And I saw a new heaven and a new earth: for the first heaven and the first earth were passed away; and there was no more sea. And God shall wipe away all tears from their eyes; and there shall be no more death, neither sorrow, nor crying, neither shall there be any

more pain: for the former things are passed away."
—REVELATION 21:1, 4

_____

_____

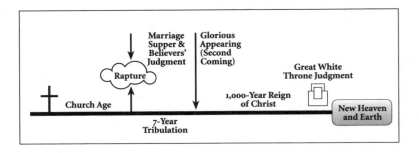

III. The _____ of God's People

"The Lord is not slack concerning his promise, as some men count slackness; but is longsuffering to us-ward, not willing that any should perish, but that all should come to repentance. But the day of the Lord will come as a thief in the night; in the which the heavens shall pass away with a great noise, and the elements shall melt with fervent heat, the earth also and the works that are therein shall be burned up. Seeing then that all these things shall be dissolved, what manner of persons ought ye to be in all holy conversation and godliness, Looking for and hasting unto the coming of the day of God, wherein the heavens being on fire shall be dissolved, and the elements shall melt with fervent heat? Nevertheless we, according to his promise, look for new heavens and a new earth, wherein dwelleth righteousness."—2 PETER 3:9–13

A. Christ's return provides a _____ in our hearts.

"Looking for that blessed hope, and the glorious appearing of the great God and our Saviour Jesus Christ;"—TITUS 2:13

_____

_____

B. Christ's return purifies the _____ of our living.

"And every man that hath this hope in him purifieth himself, even as he is pure."—1 JOHN 3:3

_____

_____

C. Christ's return promotes a _____ for souls.

_____

_____

D. Christ's return produces a _____ in our priorities.

"Now if any man build upon this foundation gold, silver, precious stones, wood, hay, stubble; Every man's work shall be made manifest: for the day shall declare it, because it shall be revealed by fire; and the fire shall try every man's work of what sort it is. If any man's work abide which he hath built thereupon, he shall receive a reward. If any man's work shall be burned, he shall suffer loss: but he himself shall be saved; yet so as by fire."—1 CORINTHIANS 3:12–15

_____

_____

Conclusion

Study Questions

1. The Lord instructed Israel to reject any prophets who failed to prophesy with accuracy (Deuteronomy 18:20–22). How can we apply this instruction to our generation?

2. Describe the rapture of believers.

3. What will happen at the Judgment Seat of Christ for believers?

4. After Christ's victory and Satan's defeat following the Tribulation, how long will Satan be bound?

5. At the conclusion of one thousand years, Satan will return to form one more revolt against Jesus Christ. What will happen after this revolt?

6. Who will stand at the Great White Throne Judgment?

7. With what promise does the book of Revelation conclude?

8. How does knowing of the prophecies to come affect your daily life?

9. If you found out that Jesus Christ was coming back tomorrow, what changes would you make in your schedule, your lifestyle, and your priorities?

Memory Verse

"Looking for that blessed hope, and the glorious appearing of the great God and our Saviour Jesus Christ;"—TITUS 2:13

Growing in the Measure of Our Faith

Key Verses

"And he gave some, apostles; and some, prophets; and some, evangelists; and some, pastors and teachers; For the perfecting of the saints, for the work of the ministry, for the edifying of the body of Christ: Till we all come in the unity of the faith, and of the knowledge of the Son of God, unto a perfect man, unto the measure of the stature of the fulness of Christ: That we henceforth be no more children, tossed to and fro, and carried about with every wind of doctrine, by the sleight of men, and cunning craftiness, whereby they lie in wait to deceive; But speaking the truth in love, may grow up into him in all things, which is the head, even Christ: From whom the whole body fitly joined together and compacted by that which every joint supplieth, according to the effectual working in the measure of every part, maketh increase of the body unto the edifying of itself in love."—EPHESIANS 4:11–16

Lesson Overview

This week's goal shifts from defining our faith to demonstrating our faith. We have focused on beliefs, and now we will focus on behaviors. The first lesson in this part of our study addresses the basics of real spiritual growth.

Introduction

_____

_____

_____

Last Six Weeks	Next Six Weeks
Defining Our Faith	Demonstrating Our Faith
Identifying: Beliefs	Identifying: Behaviors
Consideration: Our Doctrine	Consideration: Our Daily Living
Romans 10:17—**Hearing** the Word	James 1:22—**Doing** the Word

I.   The _____ of Spiritual Growth

A. Our likeness to the _____ of Christ (v. 13)

"For we dare not make ourselves of the number, or compare ourselves with some that commend themselves: but they measuring themselves by themselves, and comparing themselves among themselves, are not wise."—2 CORINTHIANS 10:12

"For whom he did foreknow, he also did predestinate to be conformed to the image of his Son, that he might be the firstborn among many brethren."—ROMANS 8:29

_____

_____

B. Our living with the _____ of Christ (v. 15b)

"And he is the head of the body, the church: who is the beginning, the firstborn from the dead; that in all things he might have the preeminence."—COLOSSIANS 1:18

_____

_____

II. The _____ of Spiritual Growth

A. _____ *leaders help us grow. (vv. 11–12)*
"*Preach the word; be instant in season, out of season; reprove, rebuke, exhort with all longsuffering and doctrine.*"—2 TIMOTHY 4:2

_____

_____

B. _____ *relationships help us grow.*
(vv. 12b, 16)
"*Iron sharpeneth iron; so a man sharpeneth the countenance of his friend.*"—PROVERBS 27:17

"*The Lord give mercy unto the house of Onesiphorus; for he oft refreshed me, and was not ashamed of my chain:*"—2 TIMOTHY 1:16

_____

_____

C. A _____ *diet helps us grow.*

_____

_____

III. The _____ of Spiritual Growth

A. _____ *in their church (v. 12)*
"*But all these worketh that one and the selfsame Spirit, dividing to **every man** severally as he will.*"
—1 CORINTHIANS 12:11

*"As **every man** hath received the gift, even so minister the same one to another, as good stewards of the manifold grace of God."*—1 Peter 4:10

_____

_____

B. _____ *in their walk (v. 14a)*
"A double minded man is unstable in all his ways."
—James 1:8

_____

_____

C. _____ *in their doctrine (v. 14b)*
"That we henceforth be no more children, tossed to and fro, and carried about with every wind of doctrine, by the sleight of men, and cunning craftiness, whereby they lie in wait to deceive;"—Ephesians 4:14

"But I fear, lest by any means, as the serpent beguiled Eve through his subtilty, so your minds should be corrupted from the simplicity that is in Christ. For if he that cometh preacheth another Jesus, whom we have not preached, or if ye receive another spirit, which ye have not received, or another gospel, which ye have not accepted, ye might well bear with him."
—2 Corinthians 11:3–4

_____

_____

D. _____ *in their communication*
"But speaking the truth in love, may grow up into him in all things, which is the head, even Christ:"
—Ephesians 4:15

_____

_____

Conclusion

_____

_____

_____

Study Questions

1. Instead of comparing yourself with others, with whom should you compare yourself regarding your Christian walk?

2. What does the term *preeminent* mean, and why is it important for Jesus Christ to be preeminent in your life?

3. Think of a spiritual leader in your life, and write one incident of when he or she helped you grow spiritually.

4. Godly, Christian friends are given to you as one of God's tools to help you grow. Write down one way you can show appreciation to one of your Christian friends for his or her example and edification.

5. According to Ephesians 4:12, the saints are to do the work of the ministry. In the next seven days, list one or more areas in which you can volunteer to serve your pastor and church family.

6. Would you consider yourself emotionally stable or unstable? Read James 1:8 and ask God for wisdom, strength, and guidance in this area.

7. According to Ephesians 4:15, how are you supposed to speak the truth?

8. Solomon said, *"Faithful are the wounds of a friend."* When a friend begins to stray from the Bible, what should your reaction be?

9. Evaluate your measure of faith. Are you a more serving, constant, and sincere Christian today than you were one month ago?

Read over your memory verse, and ask God to help you grow in grace so that in one month you can look back and measure the growth of your faith!

Memory Verse

"But grow in grace, and in the knowledge of our Lord and Saviour Jesus Christ. To him be glory both now and for ever. Amen."—2 PETER 3:18

Living Out a Model of Our Faith

Key Verses

"And ye became followers of us, and of the Lord, having received the word in much affliction, with joy of the Holy Ghost: So that ye were ensamples to all that believe in Macedonia and Achaia. For from you sounded out the word of the Lord not only in Macedonia and Achaia, but also in every place your faith to God-ward is spread abroad; so that we need not to speak any thing. For they themselves shew of us what manner of entering in we had unto you, and how ye turned to God from idols to serve the living and true God; And to wait for his Son from heaven, whom he raised from the dead, even Jesus, which delivered us from the wrath to come."
—1 THESSALONIANS 1:6–10

Lesson Overview

The Bible tells us that the faith of the Thessalonian believers was spread abroad in every place. In other words, they had become models of their faith—their faith was working its way out from the inside. Looking into Paul's description enables us to understand how we too might become models of the faith.

Introduction

_____

_____

_____

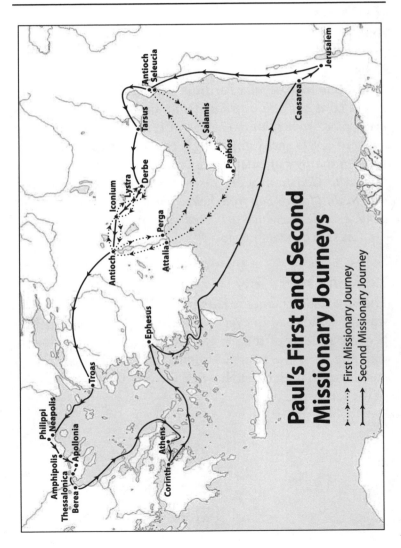

Paul's First and Second Missionary Journeys

First Missionary Journey
Second Missionary Journey

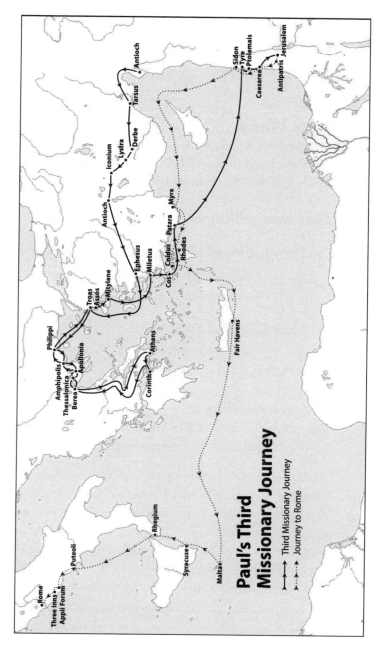

Paul's Third
Missionary Journey

→ Third Missionary Journey
····▸ Journey to Rome

"First, I thank my God through Jesus Christ for you all, that your faith is spoken of throughout the whole world."
—ROMANS 1:8

I. Theirs Was a _____ Faith

"And ye became followers of us, and of the Lord, having received the word in much affliction, with joy of the Holy Ghost:"—1 THESSALONIANS 1:6

A. They were willing to _____.

1. They followed their leadership.

"Be ye followers of me, even as I also am of Christ."—1 CORINTHIANS 11:1

2. They followed their Lord.

"Be ye therefore followers of God, as dear children;"—EPHESIANS 5:1

B. They were willing to _____.

"Yea, and all that will live godly in Christ Jesus shall suffer persecution."—2 TIMOTHY 3:12

"Blessed are they which are persecuted for righteousness' sake: for theirs is the kingdom of heaven. Blessed are ye, when men shall revile you, and persecute you, and shall say all manner of evil against you falsely, for my sake. Rejoice, and be exceeding glad: for great is your reward in heaven: for so persecuted they the prophets which were before you."—MATTHEW 5:10–12

_____

_____

II. Theirs Was a _____ Faith

"So that ye were ensamples to all that believe in Macedonia and Achaia."—1 THESSALONIANS 1:7

A. The _____ of their pattern

"Let no man despise thy youth; but be thou an example of the believers, in word, in conversation, in charity, in spirit, in faith, in purity."—1 TIMOTHY 4:12

_____

_____

B. The _____ of their pattern

"Moreover, brethren, we do you to wit of the grace of God bestowed on the churches of Macedonia; How that in a great trial of affliction the abundance of their joy and their deep poverty abounded unto the riches of their liberality. For to their power, I bear record, yea, and beyond their power they were willing of themselves; Praying us with much intreaty that we would receive the gift, and take upon us the fellowship of the ministering to the saints."—2 CORINTHIANS 8:1–4

_____

_____

III. Theirs Was a _____ Faith

"For from you sounded out the word of the Lord not only in Macedonia and Achaia, but also in every place your faith to God-ward is spread abroad; so that we need not to speak any thing."—1 THESSALONIANS 1:8

A. They witnessed with the _____.

"So then faith cometh by hearing, and hearing by the word of God."—ROMANS 10:17

_____

_____

B. They witnessed in every _____.

"Therefore they that were scattered abroad went every where preaching the word."—ACTS 8:4

_____

_____

C. They witnessed through their _____.

"Yea, a man may say, Thou hast faith, and I have works: shew me thy faith without thy works, and I will shew thee my faith by my works."—JAMES 2:18

_____

_____

IV. Theirs Was a _____ Faith

"For they themselves shew of us what manner of entering in we had unto you, and how ye turned to God from idols to serve the living and true God;"—1 THESSALONIANS 1:9

A. Their works were a result of their _____.

"But shewed first unto them of Damascus, and at Jerusalem, and throughout all the coasts of Judaea,

and then to the Gentiles, that they should repent and turn to God, and do works meet for repentance."
—ACTS 26:20

B. Their works were for the _____ and _____ God.

"What profiteth the graven image that the maker thereof hath graven it; the molten image, and a teacher of lies, that the maker of his work trusteth therein, to make dumb idols?"—HABAKKUK 2:18

V. Theirs Was a _____ Faith

"And to wait for his Son from heaven, whom he raised from the dead, even Jesus, which delivered us from the wrath to come."—1 THESSALONIANS 1:10

A. They waited with _____.

"Be patient therefore, brethren, unto the coming of the Lord. Behold, the husbandman waiteth for the precious fruit of the earth, and hath long patience for it, until he receive the early and latter rain. Be ye also patient; stablish your hearts: for the coming of the Lord draweth nigh. Grudge not one against another, brethren, lest ye be condemned: behold, the judge standeth before the door. Take, my brethren, the prophets, who have spoken in the name of the Lord, for an example of suffering affliction, and of patience. Behold, we count them happy which endure. Ye have

heard of the patience of Job, and have seen the end of the Lord; that the Lord is very pitiful, and of tender mercy."—JAMES 5:7–11

_____

_____

B. They waited with _____.
"*Looking for that blessed hope, and the glorious appearing of the great God and our Saviour Jesus Christ;*"—TITUS 2:13

_____

_____

Conclusion

_____

_____

_____

Study Questions

1. What does the term *follower* mean?

2. Name three godly examples of people you know whom you could follow, to be more like Christ.

3. What does Matthew 5:10–12 tell you about the repercussions of suffering for Christ?

4. List the qualities in *your* life that you would like another to "follow."

5. List six ways in which 1 Timothy 4:12 admonishes you to be an example.

6. According to the Bible, what does the word *repent* mean?

Has the Holy Spirit been convicting you to repent of a certain sin or weight that is besetting you? If so, bow your head now, and ask the Lord for forgiveness.

7.   Describe the works of the Thessalonian believers.

8.   How would you respond to the Prophet Habakkuk's question in Habakkuk 2:18—likening the worship of idols to a stronghold or idol in your life?

9.   If the Apostle Paul wrote a letter concerning your faith, how would he describe it?

Memory Verse

"Let no man despise thy youth; but be thou an example of the believers, in word, in conversation, in charity, in spirit, in faith, in purity."—1 TIMOTHY 4:12

Giving Out the Message of Our Faith

Key Verses

"Afterward he appeared unto the eleven as they sat at meat, and upbraided them with their unbelief and hardness of heart, because they believed not them which had seen him after he was risen. And he said unto them, Go ye into all the world, and preach the gospel to every creature. He that believeth and is baptized shall be saved; but he that believeth not shall be damned. And these signs shall follow them that believe; In my name shall they cast out devils; they shall speak with new tongues; They shall take up serpents; and if they drink any deadly thing, it shall not hurt them; they shall lay hands on the sick, and they shall recover. So then after the Lord had spoken unto them, he was received up into heaven, and sat on the right hand of God. And they went forth, and preached every where, the Lord working with them, and confirming the word with signs following. Amen."—MARK 16:14–20

Lesson Overview

We have been entrusted with a message that has the potential to change people's eternal destiny. Our message can help comfort the afflicted, convict the sinner, and challenge the believer. Our message can transform lives and touch hearts. We have the truth, and this truth must be proclaimed! Today's study will delve into the practical and biblical ways we can share the message of the Gospel.

Introduction

_____

_____

_____

I. The _____ of the Messengers
—*"they went forth"*

A. *Going forth is the _____ step.*
"They that sow in tears shall reap in joy. He that goeth forth and weepeth, bearing precious seed, shall doubtless come again with rejoicing, bringing his sheaves with him."—PSALM 126:5–6

_____

_____

B. *Going forth is an _____ step.*
"Go ye therefore, and teach all nations, baptizing them in the name of the Father, and of the Son, and of the Holy Ghost:"—MATTHEW 28:19

"And he said unto them, Go ye into all the world, and preach the gospel to every creature."—MARK 16:15

"And the lord said unto the servant, Go out into the highways and hedges, and compel them to come in, that my house may be filled."—LUKE 14:23

"Then said Jesus to them again, Peace be unto you: as my Father hath sent me, even so send I you."—JOHN 20:21

_____

_____

II. The _____ of the Messengers
—"and preached every where"

A. *The messengers were _____.*
"For we cannot but speak the things which we have seen and heard."—ACTS 4:20

_____

_____

B. *The recipients were _____.*

_____

_____

III. The _____ of the Messengers
—"the Lord working with them"

A. *He promises His _____.*

_____

_____

B. *He promises His _____.*
"I am the vine, ye are the branches: He that abideth in me, and I in him, the same bringeth forth much fruit: for without me ye can do nothing."—JOHN 15:5

_____

_____

IV. The _____ of the Messengers
—"confirming the word"

A. *Good _____ authenticate our message.*

"Let your light so shine before men, that they may see your good works, and glorify your Father which is in heaven."—MATTHEW 5:16

—————————————————————————

—————————————————————————

B. _____ *authenticates our message.*
"Now when they saw the boldness of Peter and John, and perceived that they were unlearned and ignorant men, they marvelled; and they took knowledge of them, that they had been with Jesus."—ACTS 4:13

—————————————————————————

—————————————————————————

C. _____ *authenticates our message.*
"Therefore watch, and remember, that by the space of three years I ceased not to warn every one night and day with tears."—ACTS 20:31

"And of some have compassion, making a difference:"
—JUDE 22

—————————————————————————

—————————————————————————

D. *Transformed _____ authenticate our message.*
"And be not conformed to this world: but be ye transformed by the renewing of your mind, that ye may prove what is that good, and acceptable, and perfect, will of God."—ROMANS 12:2

"Therefore if any man be in Christ, he is a new creature: old things are passed away; behold, all things are become new."—2 CORINTHIANS 5:17

—————————————————————————

—————————————————————————

E. _____ *in suffering authenticates our message.*

"Yet if any man suffer as a Christian, let him not be ashamed; but let him glorify God on this behalf. Wherefore let them that suffer according to the will of God commit the keeping of their souls to him in well doing, as unto a faithful Creator."—1 PETER 4:16, 19

_____

_____

F. _____ *words authenticate our message.*

"And all bare him witness, and wondered at the gracious words which proceeded out of his mouth. And they said, Is not this Joseph's son?"—LUKE 4:22

"Let your speech be alway with grace, seasoned with salt, that ye may know how ye ought to answer every man."—COLOSSIANS 4:6

_____

_____

G. Holy _____ *authenticates our message.*

"But as he which hath called you is holy, so be ye holy in all manner of conversation; Because it is written, Be ye holy; for I am holy."—1 PETER 1:15–16

"But ye are a chosen generation, a royal priesthood, an holy nation, a peculiar people; that ye should shew forth the praises of him who hath called you out of darkness into his marvellous light:"—1 PETER 2:9

_____

_____

Conclusion

Study Questions

1. What is the one factor that will determine whether our faith continues into the days ahead?

2. How can you perform the initial step of getting the message of Christ to others?

3. List the types of people Jesus reached with the truth.

4. Write out three verses in the Bible where the Lord promises His presence.

5. How can you obtain God's power to help you share the Gospel?

6. How can your good works authenticate the message of the Gospel?

7. How does Colossians 4:6 help you to authenticate the message of Christ?

8. To win the world to Christ, do you need to be just like the world? Use a Bible verse to help explain your answer.

9. Describe the last conversation you had with a stranger, whether it was in line at a grocery store, the bank, or even a waiter or waitress. Did you share the message of Christ?

After hearing the truths in this lesson, the next time you find yourself speaking with a stranger, remember to share the Gospel—the truth of Christ.

Memory Verse

"And he said unto them, Go ye into all the world, and preach the gospel to every creature."—MARK 16:15

Having the Faith to Surrender All

Key Verses

"And it came to pass after these things, that God did tempt Abraham, and said unto him, Abraham: and he said, Behold, here I am. And he said, Take now thy son, thine only son Isaac, whom thou lovest, and get thee into the land of Moriah; and offer him there for a burnt offering upon one of the mountains which I will tell thee of. And Abraham rose up early in the morning, and saddled his ass, and took two of his young men with him, and Isaac his son, and clave the wood for the burnt offering, and rose up, and went unto the place of which God had told him."—GENESIS 22:1–3

Lesson Overview

Today's lesson relates to demonstrating surrender, particularly in the area of our finances. We all need to be encouraged and motivated in the area of financial stewardship. There may be some who are dealing with the decision to begin tithing, to give to missions, or to participate in a special offering. This type of giving requires surrender.

Abraham willingly gave his most treasured possession; from him, we can learn that giving is a gift from God and the fruit of a surrendered heart.

Introduction

_____

_____

_____

I. The _____ to Surrender (vv. 1–2)

A. This prompting's _____ was to _____ Him.

"Then said the LORD unto Moses, Behold, I will rain bread from heaven for you; and the people shall go out and gather a certain rate every day, that I may prove them, whether they will walk in my law, or no." —EXODUS 16:4

"I speak not by commandment, but by occasion of the forwardness of others, and to prove the sincerity of your love."—2 CORINTHIANS 8:8

_____

_____

B. This prompting _____ his _____.

"Praying us with much intreaty that we would receive the gift, and take upon us the fellowship of the ministering to the saints. And this they did, not as we hoped, but first gave their own selves to the Lord, and unto us by the will of God."—2 CORINTHIANS 8:4–5

_____

_____

C. *This prompting* _____ *what was*
_____.

*"And being in Bethany in the house of Simon the leper,
as he sat at meat, there came a woman having an
alabaster box of ointment of spikenard very precious;
and she brake the box, and poured it on his head."*
—MARK 14:3

*"But with the precious blood of Christ, as of a lamb
without blemish and without spot:"*—1 PETER 1:19

_____

_____

II. The _____ of Surrender (vv. 3–10)

A. *The process involved* _____.

_____

_____

B. *The process involved* _____.
*"And the king said unto Araunah, Nay; but I will surely
buy it of thee at a price: neither will I offer burnt
offerings unto the LORD my God of that which doth cost
me nothing. So David bought the threshingfloor and
the oxen for fifty shekels of silver."*—2 SAMUEL 24:24

*"By him therefore let us offer the sacrifice of praise to
God continually, that is, the fruit of our lips giving
thanks to his name. But to do good and to communicate
forget not: for with such sacrifices God is well pleased."*
—HEBREWS 13:15–16

_____

_____

C. The process involved _____.

"*Now the just shall live by faith: but if any man draw back, my soul shall have no pleasure in him. But we are not of them who draw back unto perdition; but of them that believe to the saving of the soul.*"
—HEBREWS 10:38–39

_____

_____

D. The process involved _____ **God.**

"*Bring ye all the tithes into the storehouse, that there may be meat in mine house, and prove me now herewith, saith the* LORD *of hosts, if I will not open you the windows of heaven, and pour you out a blessing, that there shall not be room enough to receive it.*"
—MALACHI 3:10

_____

_____

III. The _____ of Surrender (vv. 11–18)

A. The promise _____ **in God's**

_____.

"*Therefore take no thought, saying, What shall we eat? or, What shall we drink? or, Wherewithal shall we be clothed? (For after all these things do the Gentiles seek:) for your heavenly Father knoweth that ye have need of all these things. But seek ye first the kingdom of God, and his righteousness; and all these things shall be added unto you.*"—MATTHEW 6:31–33

_____

_____

B. The promise _____ God's _____.

"Trust in the LORD with all thine heart; and lean not unto thine own understanding. In all thy ways acknowledge him, and he shall direct thy paths."
—PROVERBS 3:5–6

_____

_____

C. The promise _____ God's _____.

"Give, and it shall be given unto you; good measure, pressed down, and shaken together, and running over, shall men give into your bosom. For with the same measure that ye mete withal it shall be measured to you again."—LUKE 6:38

_____

_____

Conclusion

_____

_____

_____

Study Questions

1. Describe how "surrender" applies in the areas of a career, family, and finances.

2. Why does God test His children?

3. What preceded the financial giving of the Macedonian believers in 2 Corinthians 8:4–5?

4. In what ways do you struggle to fully trust God? Why?

    If the Holy Spirit brings to mind an area God still does not have control over, whether it be music, friends, work, money, etc., read Romans 12:1–3 and ask God to help you submit this area to Him.

5. In the New Testament, to what is Christian giving often related?

6. What did God ask Abraham to surrender?

7. God promises provision to those who surrender to Him. How did God provide for Abraham?

8. Abraham passed the ultimate test of faith—he was willing to sacrifice his most precious possession! Write down three of your most precious possessions.

    Are you willing to surrender these possessions if the Lord asks it of you? Read Luke 6:38, and write down the promise God makes to those who give to Him.

9. Describe one way that God has provided for you when you trusted Him.

Memory Verse

"Give, and it shall be given unto you; good measure, pressed down, and shaken together, and running over, shall men give into your bosom. For with the same measure that ye mete withal it shall be measured to you again."—LUKE 6:38

Having the Faith to Steward Our Resources

Key Verse

"He that is faithful in that which is least is faithful also in much: and he that is unjust in the least is unjust also in much. If therefore ye have not been faithful in the unrighteous mammon, who will commit to your trust the true riches? And if ye have not been faithful in that which is another man's, who shall give you that which is your own? No servant can serve two masters: for either he will hate the one, and love the other; or else he will hold to the one, and despise the other. Ye cannot serve God and mammon."—LUKE 16:10–13

Lesson Overview

Learning to be a wise steward of God's resources involves more than giving. It involves trust, faith, and a whole lot of consulting God! Whether your financial needs or resources are great or small, the crucial element is that God is the decision-maker in every area. Through His Word, God teaches us how to be good stewards of the resources He has entrusted to us.

Introduction

_____

_____

_____

I. The _____ of a Steward

A. *A steward is to _____ the owner's resources.*

1. God is the _____.

> "But who am I, and what is my people, that we should be able to offer so willingly after this sort? for all things come of thee, and of thine own have we given thee."—1 CHRONICLES 29:14

> "The earth is the LORD's, and the fulness thereof; the world, and they that dwell therein."—PSALM 24:1

> "What? know ye not that your body is the temple of the Holy Ghost which is in you, which ye have of God, and ye are not your own? For ye are bought with a price: therefore glorify God in your body, and in your spirit, which are God's."—1 CORINTHIANS 6:19–20

2. I am His _____.

B. *A steward is to _____ the owner's resources.*

> "Not because I desire a gift: but I desire fruit that may abound to your account."—PHILIPPIANS 4:17

_____

_____

II. The _____ of a Steward

"And he said also unto his disciples, There was a certain rich man, which had a steward; and the same was accused unto him that he had wasted his goods. And he called him, and said unto him, How is it that I hear this of thee? give an account of thy stewardship; for thou mayest be no longer steward. Then the steward said within himself, What shall I do? for my lord taketh away from me the stewardship: I cannot dig; to beg I am ashamed. I am resolved what to do, that, when I am put out of the stewardship, they may receive me into their houses. So he called every one of his lord's debtors unto him, and said unto the first, How much owest thou unto my lord? And he said, An hundred measures of oil. And he said unto him, Take thy bill, and sit down quickly, and write fifty. Then said he to another, And how much owest thou? And he said, An hundred measures of wheat. And he said unto him, Take thy bill, and write fourscore. And the lord commended the unjust steward, because he had done wisely: for the children of this world are in their generation wiser than the children of light."
—LUKE 16:1–8

A. The parable illustrates the steward's

_____.

"Now if any man build upon this foundation gold, silver, precious stones, wood, hay, stubble; Every man's work shall be made manifest: for the day shall declare it, because it shall be revealed by fire; and the fire shall try every man's work of what sort it is. If any man's work abide which he hath built thereupon, he shall receive a reward."—1 CORINTHIANS 3:12–14

_____

_____

B. This parable illustrates the steward's

_____.

"Give, and it shall be given unto you; good measure, pressed down, and shaken together, and running over, shall men give into your bosom. For with the same measure that ye mete withal it shall be measured to you again."—LUKE 6:38

"And, behold, I come quickly; and my reward is with me, to give every man according as his work shall be."—REVELATION 22:12

_____

_____

III. The _____ for a Steward

A. The principle of _____

"He that is faithful in that which is least is faithful also in much: and he that is unjust in the least is unjust also in much. If therefore ye have not been faithful in the unrighteous mammon, who will commit to your trust the true riches?"—LUKE 16:10–11

_____

_____

B. The principle of _____

"And if ye have not been faithful in that which is another man's, who shall give you that which is your own?"—LUKE 16:12

_____

_____

C. The principle of _____

"Lay not up for yourselves treasures upon earth, where moth and rust doth corrupt, and where thieves break through and steal: But lay up for yourselves treasures in heaven, where neither moth nor rust doth corrupt, and where thieves do not break through nor steal: For where your treasure is, there will your heart be also."—MATTHEW 6:19–21

_____

_____

D. The principle of _____

"No servant can serve two masters: for either he will hate the one, and love the other; or else he will hold to the one, and despise the other. Ye cannot serve God and mammon."—LUKE 16:13

_____

_____

Conclusion

_____

_____

_____

Study Questions

1. In life, what are the two schools of thought?

2. According to the Bible, what is the meaning of the word *steward*?

3. Who is the owner and who is the manager?

4. What principles can we learn from The Parable of the Talents?

5. How did the story of The Parable of the Unjust Steward end?

6. Just like the unjust steward, it is not too late to
    become wise in the area of stewardship. What steps
    can you take to better your stewardship of God's
    resources?

7. According to Randy Alcorn, what is one of the
    greatest roadblocks to giving?

8. According to Luke 16:13, we cannot serve both God
    and man. How does this verse apply to our resources?

9. Be sensitive to God's voice regarding stewardship. Is
    He telling you to revamp your entire financial system,
    or is He asking you to consult Him more often?
    Consider your financial state and write down what
    you believe can be changed that would best benefit
    God's resources.

Memory Verse

"Moreover it is required in stewards, that a man be found faithful."—1 CORINTHIANS 4:2

Integrating Our Faith into Our Daily Lives

Key Verses

"What doth it profit, my brethren, though a man say he hath faith, and have not works? can faith save him? If a brother or sister be naked, and destitute of daily food, And one of you say unto them, Depart in peace, be ye warmed and filled; notwithstanding ye give them not those things which are needful to the body; what doth it profit? Even so faith, if it hath not works, is dead, being alone. Yea, a man may say, Thou hast faith, and I have works: shew me thy faith without thy works, and I will shew thee my faith by my works."
—JAMES 2:14–18

Lesson Overview

Faith is a required element for the Christian life. Salvation comes through faith. But the moment of salvation is just the beginning of an entire lifetime of faith. The works we do in our daily lives either contradict or confirm the reality of our faith. There are several lessons in the book of James which illustrate how to integrate our faith into everyday living.

Introduction

_____

_____

_____

I. The _____ of Integrating Our Faith into Our Daily Lives

A. *Our actions _____ our faith.*

_____

_____

B. *Our actions _____ to our faith.*

"But I have greater witness than that of John: for the works which the Father hath given me to finish, the same works that I do, bear witness of me, that the Father hath sent me."—JOHN 5:36

_____

_____

II. The _____ for Integrating Our Faith into Our Daily Lives

"But be ye doers of the word, and not hearers only, deceiving your own selves. For if any be a hearer of the word, and not a doer, he is like unto a man beholding his natural face in a glass: For he beholdeth himself, and goeth his way, and straightway forgetteth what manner of man he was. But whoso looketh into the perfect law of

liberty, and continueth therein, he being not a forgetful hearer, but a doer of the work, this man shall be blessed in his deed."—James 1:22–25

A. We must _____ the Word of God.

"This book of the law shall not depart out of thy mouth; but thou shalt meditate therein day and night, that thou mayest observe to do according to all that is written therein: for then thou shalt make thy way prosperous, and then thou shalt have good success."
—Joshua 1:8

_____

_____

B. We must ____ something with the Word of God.

"And why call ye me, Lord, Lord, and do not the things which I say? Whosoever cometh to me, and heareth my sayings, and doeth them, I will shew you to whom he is like: He is like a man which built an house, and digged deep, and laid the foundation on a rock: and when the flood arose, the stream beat vehemently upon that house, and could not shake it: for it was founded upon a rock. But he that heareth, and doeth not, is like a man that without a foundation built an house upon the earth; against which the stream did beat vehemently, and immediately it fell; and the ruin of that house was great."—Luke 6:46–49

_____

_____

C. We must _____ in the Word of God.

"Wherefore let him that thinketh he standeth take heed lest he fall."—1 Corinthians 10:12

"Take heed unto thyself, and unto the doctrine; continue in them: for in doing this thou shalt both save thyself, and them that hear thee."—1 TIMOTHY 4:16

"Give us day by day our daily bread."—LUKE 11:3

"For which cause we faint not; but though our outward man perish, yet the inward man is renewed day by day."—2 CORINTHIANS 4:16

_____

_____

III. The _____ of Integrating Our Faith into Our Daily Lives

A. *We will _____ temptation—James 1.*

"Let no man say when he is tempted, I am tempted of God: for God cannot be tempted with evil, neither tempteth he any man: But every man is tempted, when he is drawn away of his own lust, and enticed. Then when lust hath conceived, it bringeth forth sin: and sin, when it is finished, bringeth forth death."
—JAMES 1:13–15

"There hath no temptation taken you but such as is common to man: but God is faithful, who will not suffer you to be tempted above that ye are able; but will with the temptation also make a way to escape, that ye may be able to bear it."—1 CORINTHIANS 10:13

_____

_____

B. We will _____ other people—James 2.

"My brethren, have not the faith of our Lord Jesus Christ, the Lord of glory, with respect of persons. For if there come unto your assembly a man with a gold ring, in goodly apparel, and there come in also a poor man in vile raiment; And ye have respect to him that weareth the gay clothing, and say unto him, Sit thou here in a good place; and say to the poor, Stand thou there, or sit here under my footstool: Are ye not then partial in yourselves, and are become judges of evil thoughts? Hearken, my beloved brethren, Hath not God chosen the poor of this world rich in faith, and heirs of the kingdom which he hath promised to them that love him?"—JAMES 2:1–5

"Be kindly affectioned one to another with brotherly love; in honour preferring one another; Not slothful in business; fervent in spirit; serving the Lord; Rejoicing in hope; patient in tribulation; continuing instant in prayer; Distributing to the necessity of saints; given to hospitality. Bless them which persecute you: bless, and curse not. Rejoice with them that do rejoice, and weep with them that weep. Be of the same mind one toward another. Mind not high things, but condescend to men of low estate. Be not wise in your own conceits."
—ROMANS 12:10–16

_____

_____

C. We will _____ our tongues—James 3.

"Even so the tongue is a little member, and boasteth great things. Behold, how great a matter a little fire kindleth! And the tongue is a fire, a world of iniquity: so is the tongue among our members, that it defileth the

whole body, and setteth on fire the course of nature; and it is set on fire of hell. For every kind of beasts, and of birds, and of serpents, and of things in the sea, is tamed, and hath been tamed of mankind: But the tongue can no man tame; it is an unruly evil, full of deadly poison. Therewith bless we God, even the Father; and therewith curse we men, which are made after the similitude of God. Out of the same mouth proceedeth blessing and cursing. My brethren, these things ought not so to be."—JAMES 3:5–10

_____

_____

D. We will _____ pride—James 4.

"But he giveth more grace. Wherefore he saith, God resisteth the proud, but giveth grace unto the humble. Be afflicted, and mourn, and weep: let your laughter be turned to mourning, and your joy to heaviness. Humble yourselves in the sight of the Lord, and he shall lift you up."—JAMES 4:6, 9, 10

"And whosoever shall exalt himself shall be abased; and he that shall humble himself shall be exalted."
—MATTHEW 23:12

"Likewise, ye younger, submit yourselves unto the elder. Yea, all of you be subject one to another, and be clothed with humility: for God resisteth the proud, and giveth grace to the humble. Humble yourselves therefore under the mighty hand of God, that he may exalt you in due time:"—1 PETER 5:5–6

_____

_____

E. We will _____ on prayer—James 5.

"Is any sick among you? let him call for the elders of the church; and let them pray over him, anointing him with oil in the name of the Lord: And the prayer of faith shall save the sick, and the Lord shall raise him up; and if he have committed sins, they shall be forgiven him. Confess your faults one to another, and pray one for another, that ye may be healed. The effectual fervent prayer of a righteous man availeth much."—JAMES 5:14–16

"Ask, and it shall be given you; seek, and ye shall find; knock, and it shall be opened unto you: For every one that asketh receiveth; and he that seeketh findeth; and to him that knocketh it shall be opened. Or what man is there of you, whom if his son ask bread, will he give him a stone? Or if he ask a fish, will he give him a serpent? If ye then, being evil, know how to give good gifts unto your children, how much more shall your Father which is in heaven give good things to them that ask him?"—MATTHEW 7:7–11

_____

_____

Conclusion

_____

_____

_____

Study Questions

1. What is the theme for the entire book of James?

2. Define the word *integrate*.

3. In your own words, explain this statement: "Salvation is not the *end* of the Christian life, it is just the *beginning*."

4. What resources does God give us to help us integrate our faith and our works?

5. What happens to the one in James 1:25 who "*continueth therein*"?

6. List the five results of integrating our faith into our daily lives.

7. Name one person to whom you can show kindness today. Write out the act of kindness, and include the time you plan to act upon it.

8. The Bible says that we have not because we ask not. Begin to pray specifically for a need that no one else knows about, rely solely on prayer, and see how God answers!

9. The purpose of prayer is not to be frustrated spiritually, but to discern the mind of God through our prayers. Read John 17:21 and ask God to help you become one with Him.

Memory Verse

"Yea, a man may say, Thou hast faith, and I have works: shew me thy faith without thy works, and I will shew thee my faith by my works."—JAMES 2:18

For additional Christian
growth resources visit
www.strivingtogether.com